Kampfpanzer IV • TIGER I

Horst Scheibert

The drawings on the inside front and back covers come from the covers of Service Instructions 656/27, the "Tiger Book." They quickly show the effective (red) and danger (green) areas of enemy tanks in 1943.

In this volume there are numerous quotations from the Tiger Book. With their combination of photos, humorous drawings, texts and prose, sometimes in army jargon, they are a break from the previous type of instruction books. But they were a great success with the soldiers and resulted in better training results than did the earlier instructions and memoranda. This book is still unique in its field today.

SCHIFFER MILITARY HISTORY
Atglen, Pennsylvania

Translated from the Germanby Dr. Edward Force,
Central Connecticut State University.

Library of Congress Catalog Number: 91-62746

Printed in China.
ISBN: 978-0-88740-352-1

This title was originally published under the title,
Kampfpanzer IV - Tiger 1,
by Podzun-Pallas Verlag, Friedberg.

Published by Schiffer Publishing Ltd.
4880 Lower Valley Road
Atglen, PA 19310
Phone: (610) 593-1777
FAX: (610) 593-2002
E-mail: Info@schifferbooks.com.
Visit our web site at: www.schifferbooks.com
Please write for a free catalog.
This book may be purchased from the publisher.
Please include $5.00 postage.
Try your bookstore first.

In Europe, Schiffer books are distributed by:
Bushwood Books
6 Marksbury Ave.
Kew Gardens, Surrey TW9 4JF
England
Phone: 44 (0)20 8392-8585
FAX: 44 (0)20 8392-9876
E-mail: info@bushwoodbooks.co.uk
www.bushwoodbooks.co.uk

This photo makes clear the size, strength, might, but also the angular form of the Tiger. Despite its vertical armored surfaces, enemy tanks could have relatively little effect on it in 1943; their weapons had only a slight effect on its 100-mm front armor.

Panzer IV - Tiger I

Only late, and as results on the battlefields of Russia in 1941 were to prove, too late, was the construction of heavy tanks advocated. This resulted in a too-quick decision with the resulting disadvantages, and finally too meager production. And training suffered too.

The Tiger I, shown here, first saw service at the end of August 1942 (Unit 502) near Leningrad, in December of 1942 (Unit 501) in Tunis, North Africa, and January 1943 (Unit 503) near Rostov on the Don. Its first major action came in July of 1943 in Operation "Citadel" (Kursk), in which 146 Tiger I tanks took part. After that it saw service on all fronts, though in small numbers.

The crews were not always made up of old experienced tank soldiers. Often they were young retrainees from other service arms and young replacements; only individuals — mostly officers and older NCO's — came from the replacement units of the already existing Panzer regiments, for whom the Panther (Panzer V) was reserved. This led to disappointment among the old panzer men.

The training center was the barracks of Panzer Regiment 11 in Paderborn, along with the nearby Senne training camp. There are scarcely any members of Tiger units who did not get to know this area. The units were numbered 501 to 510. They were independent units that were put into action by the high command at vital points. In addition, the three SS Panzer corps gained Tiger units, and the *Grossdeutschland* volunteer division of the army was given a Tiger company, which was later enlarged into a unit. Unit 502 was later renumbered 511, 503 joined the *Feldherrnhalle* Panzer Division, and 509 went to the Führer Escort (Begleit) Division.

Technical Data

Version	Tiger I, Type E, Sd.Kfz. 181
Manufacturer (final assembly)	Henschel & Son
Fighting weight	56.9 tons
Crew	5 men
Armament (gun, caliber, length)	1 88mm KwK 36 L/56
Turret machine gun	1 MG 34, 7.92 mm
Bow (radioman's) machine gun	1 MG 34, 7.92 mm
Machine pistol	1 MP 40, 9 mm
Antitank & explosive shells	92
Machine gun ammunition	3920-4500
Machine pistol ammunition	192
Antitank shell weight	10 kg
Muzzle velocity	810 meters per second
Penetration at 500 meters	140 mm
1000 meters	122 mm
1500 meters	108 mm
2000 meters	92 mm
2500 meters	82 mm
Armor thickness, hull	100/66 mm
front	100/80 mm
lower side	60/90 mm
upper side	80/90 mm
rear	82/82 mm
hull top	26 mm
hull bottom	26 mm
turret front	110/90 mm
turret side	80/90 mm
turret rear	80/90 mm
turret top	26/0-9 mm
Top speed	38-45 kph
Sustained speed, road	ca. 20 kph
off-road	ca. 15 kph
Range: road	ca. 100-110 km

off-road	ca. 60 km
Fuel capacity	534 liters
Fuel consumption: road	ca. 500-534 liters/100 km
off-road	ca. 900-935 liters/100 km
Ground pressure	1088 kg/cc
Performance (depending on motor and rpm)	12.3 HP/ton (10.5)
Ground clearance	47 cm
Ditch spanning ability	2.30 meters
Climbing ability	0.80 meters
Climbing ability: gradient	35 degrees
Fording ability	1.20 meters
With diving equipment	4.00 meters
Overall length, gun forward	8.241 meters
Overall length, gun aft	8.350 meters
Overall length without gun	6.200 meters
Gun overhang to front	2.040 meters
Running gear length	3.605 meters
Track width overall	3.705 meters
Track width over chains	3.560 meters
Track width	2.822 meters
Marching tracks	0.725 meters
Shipping tracks	0.520 meters
Hull width	1.800 meters
Turret rail diameter	1.790 meters
Overall height	2.880 meters (3.00 m)
Firing height	2.195 meters
Motor and gearbox	Tiger I
Motor (Otto type)	Maybach HL 230 P 45
Car I – 250 m. motor	Maybach HL 210 P 45
Performance at 2500 rpm	600 HP
Performance at 3000 rpm	700 HP
Cylinders	V 12
Displacement/cooling	23,880 (21,353), water
Gearbox	Olvar 40 12 16 pre-selector
Number of gears	8 forward, 4 reverse
Hull and turret	Self-carrying armored hull, armored superstructure with rotating turret driven by motor of vehicle

2 tracks of 96 links each (130 mm per link)
Drive wheels forward, leading wheels aft
8 large 3-part road wheels, alternating order, on each side
Total 48 road wheels
2 torsion bars per three road wheels
Hydraulic two-wheel; steering by steering wheel
Drive wheels have Argus hydraulic disc brakes

Aiming optics	T Z F 9 B
Aiming gear	1 circular control
Communication gear sender and receiver	1 on-board circuit, UKW

(Some command tanks with special equipment: no turret machine gun. Loader also serves as second radioman.

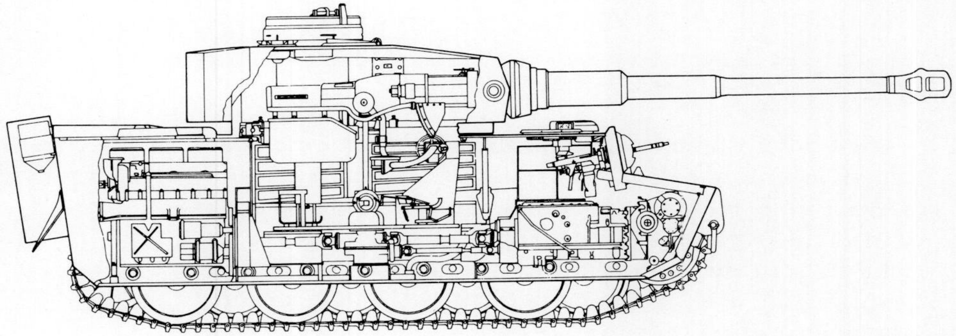

Production

It was built only by the Henschel Works from 1942 to 1945 and designated Special Motor Vehicle (Sd.Kfz.) 181.

In all, a total of 1,355 of Type E (the others were just single prototypes), including the armored command car version (which differs only in having a raised radio antenna) were built.

These photos and the two on the next page were taken in an assembly hall of the Henschel Works in Kassel. Above and right, the raw hulls without running gear, turret and weapons can be seen. The turret rail (seen at the right in the right photo) was machined with special equipment, and (in the same picture) the axle mounts for the running gear were installed.

Both pictures show the assembly of the motor, gearbox and running gear. Here the hulls are on an assembly line. The motor is a Maybach (HL 210 P 45) 12-cylinder carburetor engine producing 650 HP. The gearbox is also made by Maybach and is a semi-automatic forward transmission with 8 forward and 4 reverse gears.

Right: Before the turret is mounted, the Tiger receives its complete running gear, so that it can move. The teeth of the drive wheels can be seen clearly in the picture.

Below: This picture shows the arrangement of the road wheels. There are four rows of four wheels each, in which the middle rows consist of double wheels. In all, the Tiger has eight axles with 24 road wheels. This photo also shows the great width of the tracks (combat tracks: 725 mm, chipping tracks (photo): 520 mm.

This photo shows "Takt 8." This step is the mounting of the turret on the almost complete hull. The outer road wheels are still missing from the running gear. They were added only with the combat tracks.

Rail Transport

A Tiger I moves from a fixed loading ramp onto a special flatcar of the Reichsbahn. One of the Tiger's outer road wheels is missing, and the Zimmerite covering (against magnetic mines) is recognizable.

Motto:
Even General Guderian
Sometimes rides the railroad.
(from the Tiger Book)

Moral:
Loading is child's play
For him who knows the way.
(from the Tiger book)

Another Tiger rolls from one flatcar to another. It has its gun turned to a 6:00 (backward) position) to make more room. The sheet-metal box on the back of the turret is easy to see. The crew kept their equipment in it, since there was little room inside. Interesting in both photos is the fact that the combat tracks have been put on (the Tiger has its outer road wheels). This was done in exceptional cases for single-track transport or when the other track could be closed. The shipping tracks belonged to the SSymS special flatcar.

Marching

Motto:
The Tiger is, when you think about it,
A vehicle that steers just fine.
(from the Tiger Book)

Moral:
Like everything one may do but doesn't have to,
Driving is usually a great pleasure.
(from the Tiger Book)

Both photos were taken during the service of the heavy Panzer Unit 501 in Tunis in 1943.In the upper picture, a Horch personnel car (company chief's car) is beside the Tiger. By the tactical marking on its front fender, it belonged to a Panzer grenadier unit. The 88mm gun of the Tiger has a protector over the muzzle brake to keep out dust.

Left: A Tiger I with the symbol (two crossed keys) of the 1st SS Panzer Corps. It was carried on the right (as here) or left front plate. This tank, unlike the other, shows the rippled Zimmerite covering.

A Tiger of a heavy army tank unit at a stop on the march. Since the Tigers have not been put under cover, the camouflage is very meager and the crew is at ease, the danger from the air is not very great — thus this picture probably was taken on the eastern front in 1943.

Schwere Panzerabteilung 502
1942 – 1945

Kämpfte in:

RUSSLAND (NORDABSCHNITT)
KURLAND – OSTPREUSSEN

Above: A Tiger I at a stop on the march. The launchers for fog bombs can be seen on the upper rim of the hull and the turret, the sides of which are also protected by extra chains. As of 1942 at the latest, tank crews also wore steel helmets when they looked out of the tank while in contact with the enemy.

Left: A Tiger in a preparation area. The time is used for washing oneself and one's personal equipment. The 3:00 position of the gun suggests a securing assignment in this direction, since the barrel is somewhat camouflaged.

Here a Tiger is loaded with ammunition and fueled. The shells come from long wooden crates, the fuel from barrels.

The Tiger Book

The Tiger Book was something completely new when it appeared (August 1, 1943) and was a very successful instruction book. Its mottos and morals were widely used in everyday service.

After showing some excerpts on this page, two original full pages of instructions will follow, to show their composition.

Motto:
Oh friend, there are two sides to "Sprit",
Sometimes you drive, sometimes you fly with it.

Sprit is a fuel
When it is vaporized and, mixed with air, is burned in small quantities, it drives the 60-ton Tiger down the road by a lot of little explosions, as a child does with a tire using a lot of little pushes.
With one liter in the tank you can drive 200 meters. The striking power of a giant is in it, but spread over half a minute, it acts like a massage, and the Tiger likes that.

Sprit is an explosive
But if the same liter flows not into the carburetor but into the hull, then it vaporizes from the motor's heat, the gas mixes with the swirling air and is suddenly ignited by a spark or by heat.
This liter blows up your Tiger in such a way that the motor hood, with the roof of your compartment, is blown higher than you can throw a stone. The giant's power unites in a single knockout punch, and even a Tiger can't stand that.

Motto: Oh Freund, zwei Seiten hat der Sprit.
Mal fährst Du und mal fliegst Du mit.

Sprit

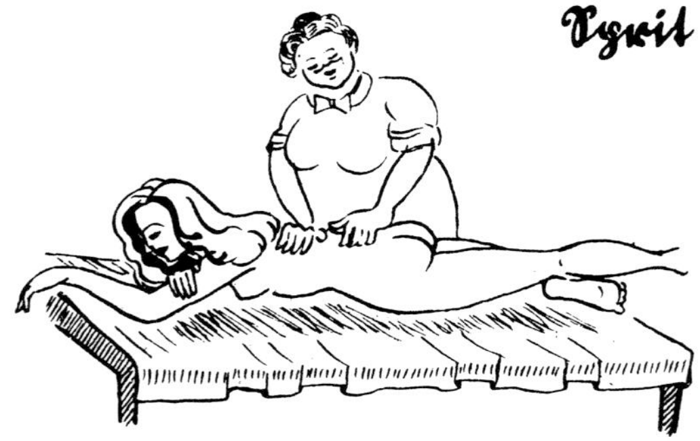

Sprit ist ein Kraftstoff

Wenn er vergast und mit Luft gemischt in kleinen Mengen entzündet wird, treibt er den Tiger mit seinen 60 Tonnen durch lauter kleine Explosionen über die Straße, wie ein Kind einen Reifen durch lauter kleine Puffe.

Mit 1 Liter im Tank kannst Du 200 m weit fahren. Es steckt die Schlagkraft eines Riesen darin, aber sie wirkt über eine halbe Minute verteilt wie eine Massage, und das hat der Tiger gern.

Sprit ist ein Sprengstoff

Fließt derselbe Liter aber, statt in den Vergaser, in die Wanne, dann vergast er durch die Motorwärme, das Gas mischt sich mit der wirbelnden Luft und wird durch einen Funken oder Hitze auf einmal gezündet.

Dieser Liter sprengt Deinen Tiger so, daß die Motorklappe mit Deinem Hausdach höher davonwirbelt, als Du einen Stein werfen kannst. Die Riesenkraft ballt sich in einen einzigen k. o. zusammen und den hält auch ein Tiger nicht aus.

Darum:

Right: Technical service to a Tiger that shows a rather unusual paint pattern on the front of the hull and the gun barrel. Part of the motor hood is raised.

Below: The commander in the turret, as seen by the gunner.

Keep the tank cap tight but the air vent open.
Otherwise the motor won't take fuel in.
Keep fuel containers and hoses clean. Don't remove the strainer.
Otherwise the gauges and fuel lines will get dirty. You can have big trouble with both.
Clean dust and water off gauges, don't damage connections, rather replace them, put in clean ones.
Tighten bolts firmly.
Otherwise the Tiger will burn or explode.

Therefore: Fill it — but don't spill it.
Otherwise the Tiger will burn or explode.
Attention! When the fuel runs out — immediately switch to reserve;
when the reserve runs out — immediately stop and turn off the motor, a 30-second job.
Otherwise the fuel pumps and lines will be emptied, and after refueling you'll get no fuel: Unscrew air filter and housing, remove hollow screws in the carburetor, let electric pump run until fuel comes (don't let it overrun). Put everything back together.
One hour's work!

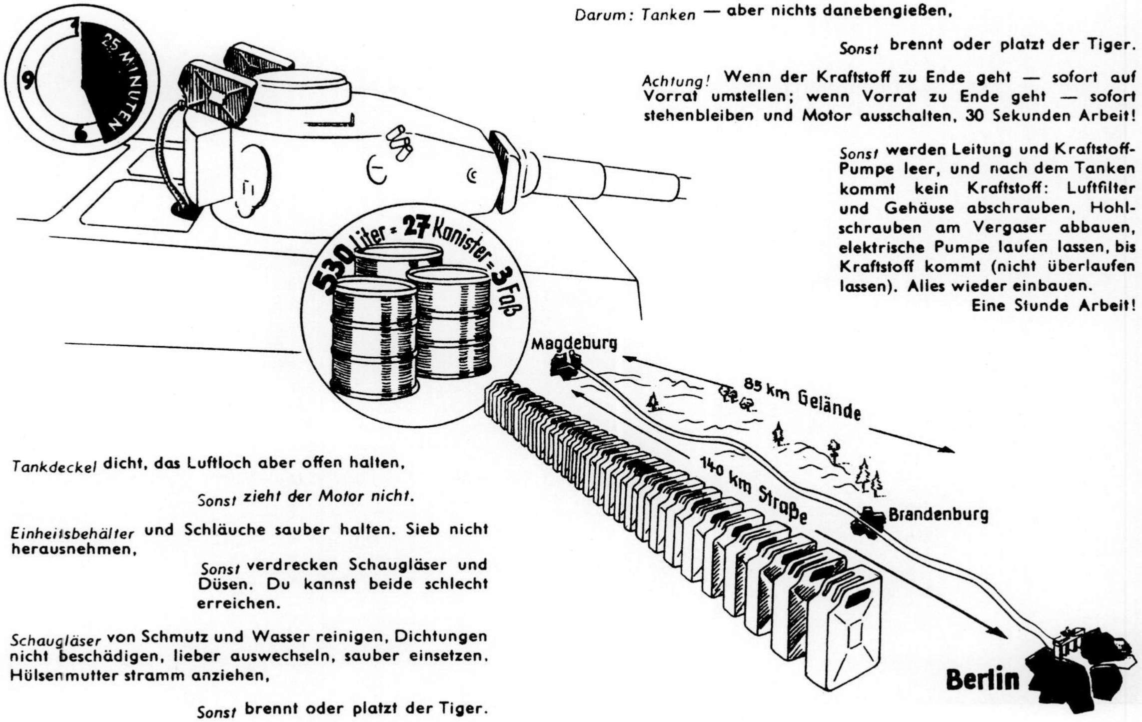

Darum: Tanken — aber nichts danebengießen,

Sonst brennt oder platzt der Tiger.

Achtung! Wenn der Kraftstoff zu Ende geht — sofort auf Vorrat umstellen; wenn Vorrat zu Ende geht — sofort stehenbleiben und Motor ausschalten, 30 Sekunden Arbeit!

Sonst werden Leitung und Kraftstoff-Pumpe leer, und nach dem Tanken kommt kein Kraftstoff: Luftfilter und Gehäuse abschrauben, Hohlschrauben am Vergaser abbauen, elektrische Pumpe laufen lassen, bis Kraftstoff kommt (nicht überlaufen lassen). Alles wieder einbauen.
Eine Stunde Arbeit!

Tankdeckel dicht, das Luftloch aber offen halten,

Sonst zieht der Motor nicht.

Einheitsbehälter und Schläuche sauber halten. Sieb nicht herausnehmen,

Sonst verdrecken Schaugläser und Düsen. Du kannst beide schlecht erreichen.

Schaugläser von Schmutz und Wasser reinigen, Dichtungen nicht beschädigen, lieber auswechseln, sauber einsetzen. Hülsenmutter stramm anziehen,

Sonst brennt oder platzt der Tiger.

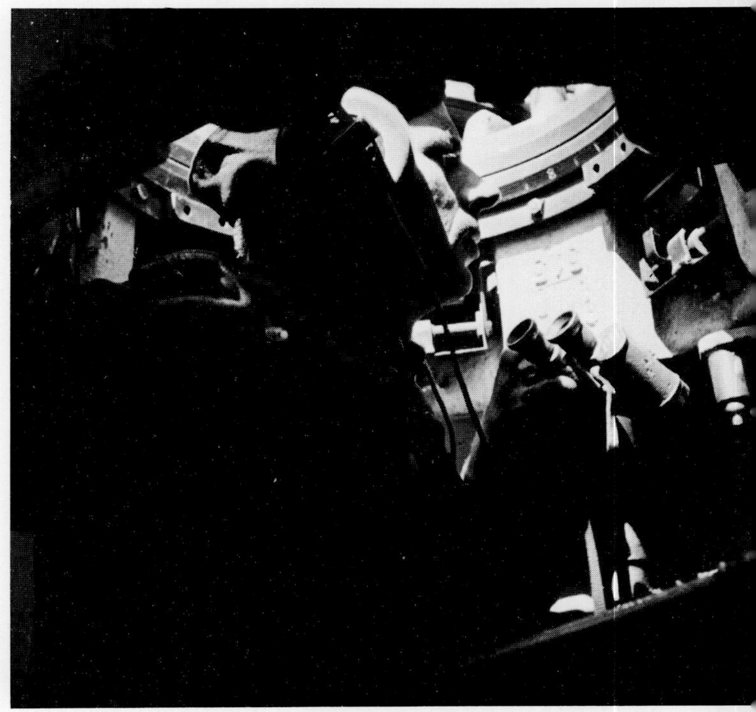

Winter

Loading ammunition in winter. Both photos show that on the steppes in winter, only a completely white-painted tank provides good camouflage. Paint jobs like those shown here probably were sufficient to disguise the contours in overgrown country, but not on a white carpet of snow.

Motto:
The way Max Schmeling throws his right,
You throw the shells when in a fight.
(from the Tiger Book)

The same applies to the uniform. There was a wide variety of winter clothing — several types can be seen in these photos: improvised or captured snow jackets, German-issue field jackets, including the two-sided type, the white side of which soon became gray (note the two soldiers on the Tiger above) that it scarcely served as camouflage any more.

Right: As one can tell by the umbrella antenna (right, this Tiger is a command tank. If immediate contact with the enemy was not expected, the driver — as here — usually had his hatch open for better ventilation. The crew are armed with 9 mm pistols, usually carried in the jacket so as not to get caught in the turret. The way it is worn in the photo is rare.

Moral:
The right estimation often does not
Hit the target, as we hope.
(from the Tiger Book)

A well-camouflaged Tiger under fresh snow secures a road out of a village. This Tiger has already lost its side track cover — which consisted only of screwed-on sheet metal.

Left: Tigers on the march. Intervals of over 50 meters were used chiefly in the west, since the danger of enemy air attack was greater there than in the east. Probably having learned from experience, this Tiger has its towline ready on the shackles.

Below: The officer on the Tiger's turret wears the German Cross in gold. He was honored for repeated bravery in combat (eight Iron Cross I awards was the standard for officers). Since it shows a big swastika, the soldiers called it the "party emblem for the nearsighted" or the "fried egg." But it was purely a medal for bravery and not — as often claimed — a party medal. The Panzer men usually wore in embroidered form, sewn on, so it would not get torn off when climbing into or out of a tank.

As can be seen by the bent sheet metal of the track covers, the damaged front road wheel and the damage above the cooking utensils, this tank is an old campaigner. In addition to the German cross on the hull, it has another on the turret (not customary). The "lunch box" (formerly an ammunition box) is on the bow — presumably the crew has just been supplied with food.

Division emblems

Großdeutschland

SS-Division
Leibstandarte Adolf Hitler

I. SS-Panzerkorps (LAH)

Tiger tanks were generally used by independent heavy tank units with numbers 501 to 510. In addition, they were supplied to the elite (volunteer) divisions of the army (*Grossdeutschland*) and the Waffen-SS (*LAH* = *Leibstandarte Adolf Hitler*). *Grossdeutschland* (*GD*) had grown from a regiment (French campaign) to the Panzer Corps *GD* by 1945, as had the *LAH*. The "Dietrich" key as a division emblem of the *LAH*, later in doubled form for the 1st SS Corps (*LAH*) represents the leader of this large unit, Sepp Dietrich. Both corps, though, existed more completely on paper than in actual fact. The continuing crises of 1944 no longer allowed complete establishment, training and equipping.

The differences between these two photos are interesting. The tank at right is painted in tropical sand tan. It can also be recognized as a Tiger for North Africa by the Feifel air cleaner at the rear, which does the job of keeping dust and other dirt out of the motor. This Tiger has a bigger cross emblem than the one below, which saw service in Europe. This is shown not only by the camouflage paint but also by the lack of an air cleaner. Like all post-1944 Tigers, it also lacks fog launchers.

The Tiger in the picture at left is followed by a VW Schwimmwagen. While berets were worn — also by officers — from 1939 to 1941, the black Schiffchen fore-and-aft cap took precedence afterward, followed in 1944 by the black mountain cap and the gray field cap (also worn by officers without silver braid).

An ideally camouflaged Tiger for winter warfare — probably painted with white body paint. This paint was very rarely seen because it was hard to remove in the spring and had to be painted over. The crew is not following their Tiger's good example. The NCO at left wears a black mountain cap, the Obergefreite in the middle wears a Schiffchen with a head protector (an olive elastic knitted ring usually pulled over the ears), and the soldier at right wears black work clothes.

Schwere Panzerabteilung 504
1943 – 1945

Kämpfte in:

TUNESIEN
SIZILIEN
ITALIEN

Schwere Panzerabteilung 505
1943 – 1945

Kämpfte in:

RUSSLAND (MITTELABSCHNITT)
OSTPREUSSEN

Schwere Panzerabteilung 506
1943 - 1945

Kämpfte in:

RUSSLAND (SÜDABSCHNITT)-POLEN
ARDENNEN-RUHRGEBIET

Schwere Panzerabteilung 507
1943 - 1945

Kämpfte in:

RUSSLAND (MITTELABSCHNITT)
POLEN

This Tiger has its number on the gun barrel (rare!). No cross emblem can be seen, but instead the emblem of Unit 505. The bar on the side of the hull is interesting — it is for use when stuck in a swamp. The side-by-side appearance of the dying cavalry with the rising technology — and yet they are related, for the Panzer troops developed out of the cavalry — always brings back memories.

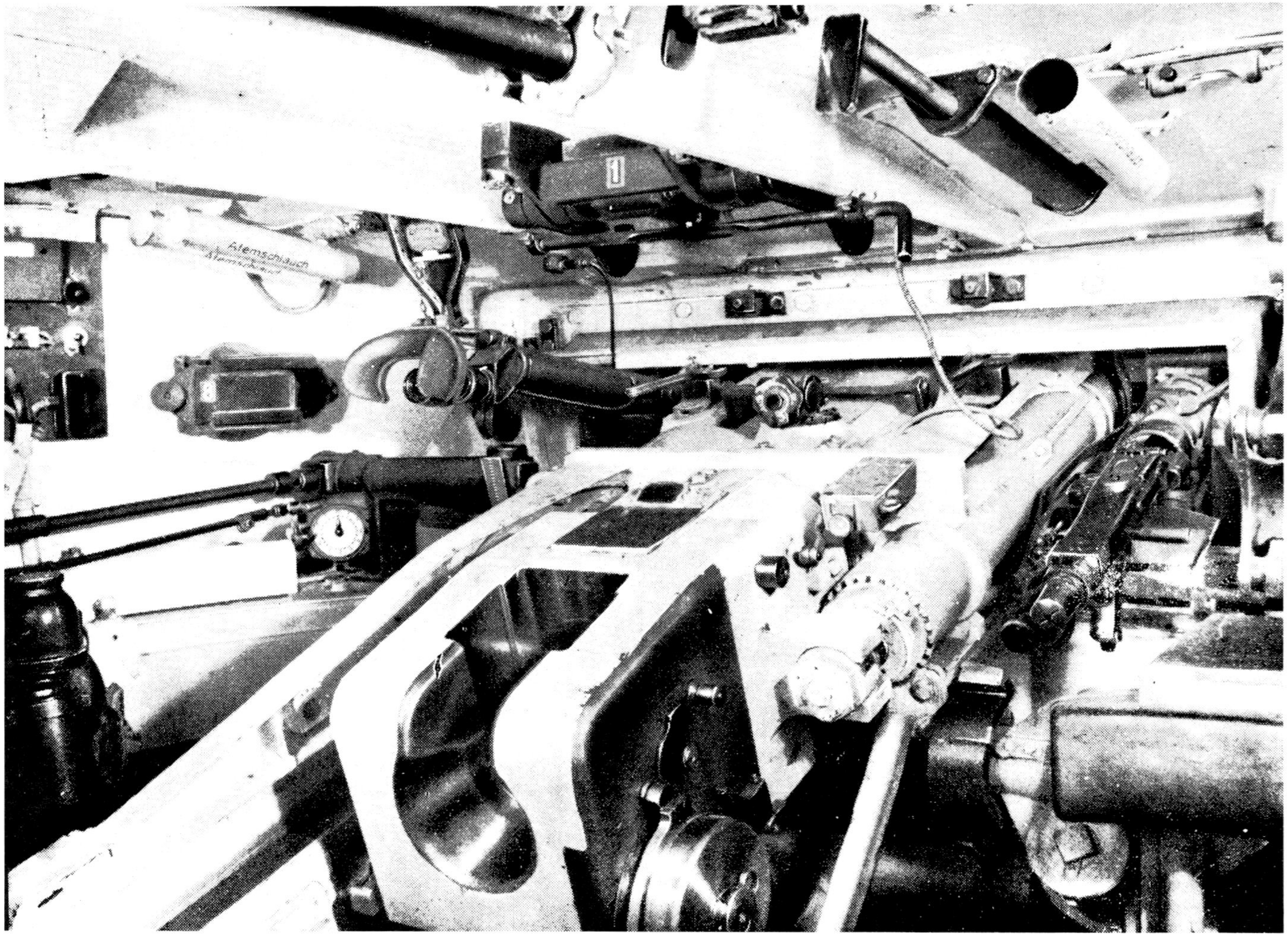

Inside the turret. At left before the easily seen optics (with forehead protector) is the gunner's seat. Behind him, on a higher plane — with his head at the level of the panoramic periscope — sits the commander, and at right, with his back to the machine gun, is the loader. His back cushion is easy to see here at the right side of the picture. All the seats can be adjusted as to height.

Above: This photo clearly shows the double optics and the two handwheels for raising the gun and turning the turret.

Upper right: Here the loader's seat can be seen.

Right: A view of the driver's seat, steering wheel and instrument panel. The large dial shows the engine speed.

The same tank is shown at left and below. The Tiger is on blocks over a makeshift pit with the right track removed to allow work on the axles or road wheels. The towline is still attached to the front shackle — presumably because the tank was towed in.

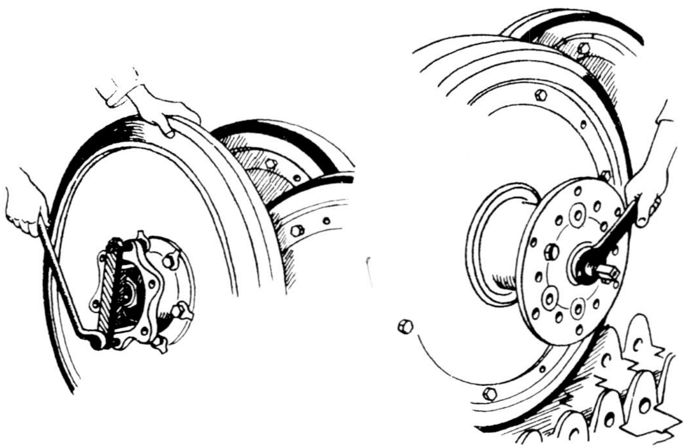

Changing a road wheel with special tools.

Right: Changing a road wheel. Below: Mounting the track. Like all Tiger parts it was heavy and required hard work.

Below: Drawings of road-wheel, drive-wheel or flange changes.

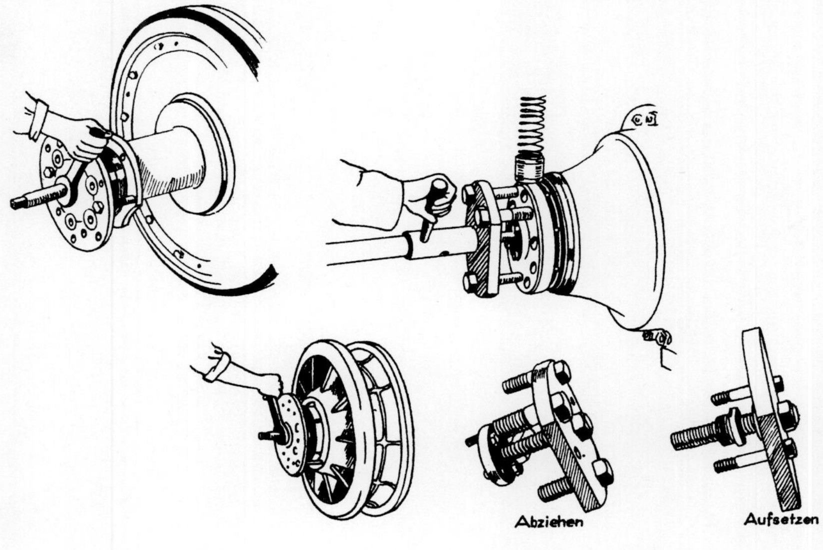

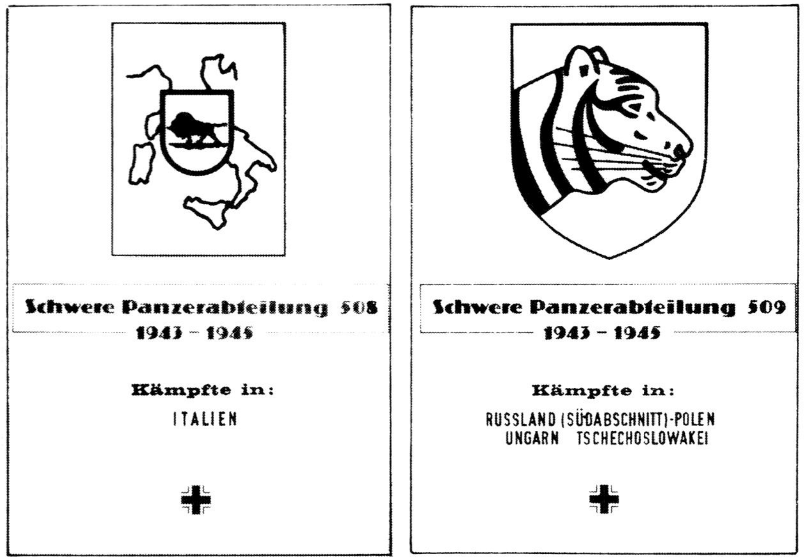

Two more emblems of army Tiger units.

Left: Here the size and weight of the Tiger's tracks are easy to see. Once the work has reached this point, it can be drawn over the road wheels by a line fastened to the drive wheel and then pulled together with the help of a chain wrench and fastened by a bolt (easily seen here).

Motto:
One thinks, when a track chain rips,
If only I'd looked after it!
(from the Tiger Book)

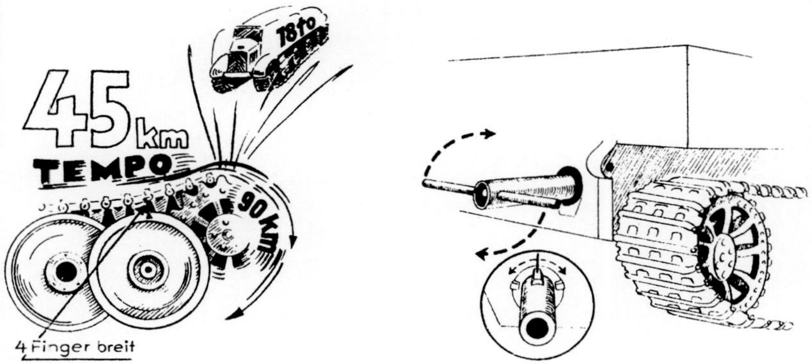

Upper left: The drawings show the speed of the track at a road speed of 45 kph, the necessary track tension, its installation (drawing at right) and weight (18 tons!) with which a too-loose track hits the drive wheel.

Above: Track damage — an outer road wheel is missing too — all of the road wheels have to roll together. Trouble had to be watched out for particularly in winter and in mud season.

Left: The left profile of a Tiger covered with Zimmerite. There were no uniform rules for the location, color and size of numbers. Almost every unit had its own system.

Combat

Left: A Tiger I in Russia. It has already hooked up its towline, and is missing an outer road wheel from its left running gear. The cannon projecting far out over the bow was often a hindrance in towns.

The two pictures below show Tigers in combat, below along with Panzer-grenadiers (in the foreground). The distance between tanks in combat became ever greater until the war ended.

Right: A broken-down Tiger in Italy — presumably with technical problems. It is camouflaged because Allied air superiority in that area was great, the weapons are protected with dust covers, and the towlines are just being attached.

Specialists discuss repairs. At left a mechanic from the repair troop (I-Trupp), at right a crew member.

Meeting in the woods — a terrain that Tigers tried to avoid, in the northern part of the eastern front near Leningrad, though, Tiger Unit 502 could not avoid it.

**Motto:
With calmness,
alertness and sense —
The rescue is soon
accomplished.
(from the Tiger Book)**

**Moral:
A rescue is indeed
very moving,
But unfortunately
necessary.
(From the Tiger Book)**

A damaged Tiger is towed by another through a Balka (dry stream bed filled up with meltwater from snow).

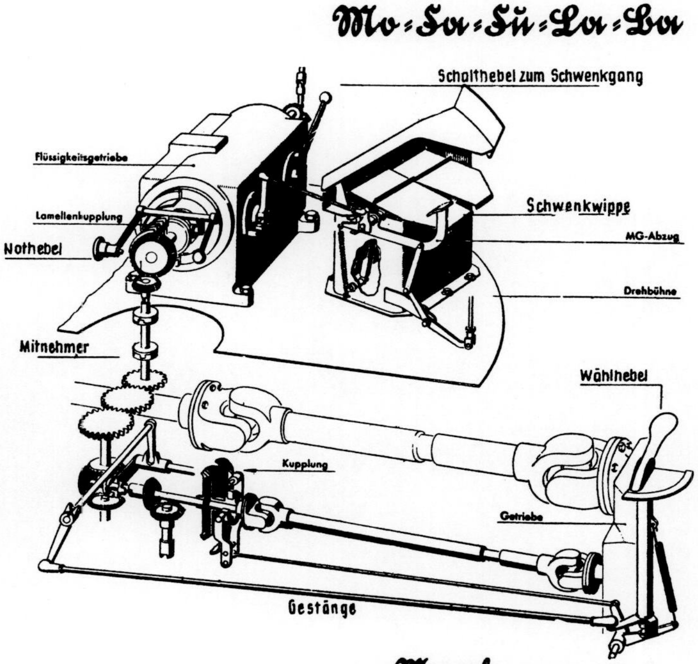

Gearbox, clutch and linkage.

Above, like a fully armored knight, threatening, and ready to take up any battle. The bracket on the turret for an anti-aircraft machine gun is noteworthy. These brackets were attached to the Tigers used in the west in 1944. On the right of the Tiger is the emblem of the 1st SS Panzer Corps.

Left: A Tiger in combat in the northern sector of the eastern front. To its right is a destroyed Russian tank that, because of its two turret hatches was nicknamed "Mickey Mouse" by the soldiers.

The view from the driver's seat.

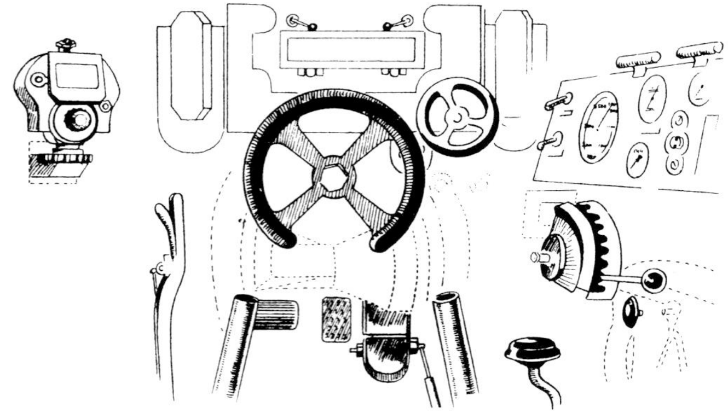

Above and right: Panzer-grenadiers of an SS division advance along with Tigers, which were first used in large numbers here, during Operation "Citadel" (summer 1943), which was intended to straighten the bulge in the front at Kursk. In this operation, though, more Tigers dropped out with technical troubles (teething problems and too-hastily trained crews) than were shot down by the enemy.

Right: Another photo of heavy (Tiger) Panzer Unit 502 in action near Leningrad. In the foreground is a Spanish rider obstacle, part of a position system. The denuded trees show that battle has raged here for some time.

Below: A Tiger in the steppes; at left a heavy enemy shell has struck. The Tiger's turret hatch is open. The reasons are: Better ventilation in the fighting compartment, hearing what is happening on the battlefield, and no substitute for a quick look around from the turret. The turret hatch was closed only where close combat with the enemy was to be expected.

Left: Tigers on the march in Italy, 1944. For the soldiers, particularly those of the infantry units, the sight of it was always an experience — and a reassuring one — and thus they were always watched with the greatest interest.

The motor had four double carburetors, the second section only opening at engine speeds of 1900 rpm or more.

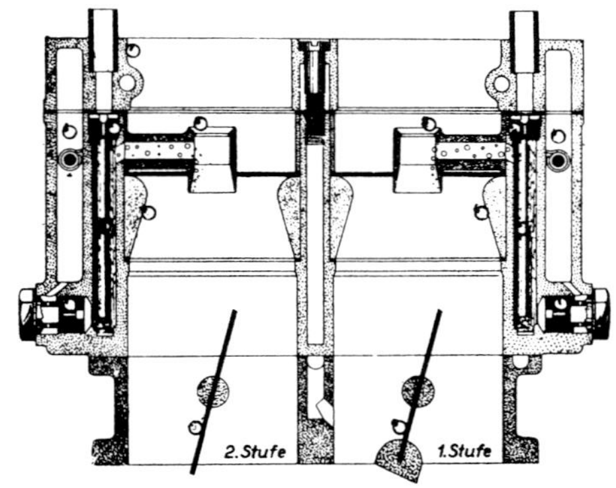

Moral:
When your engine bucks and snorts,
It's the carburetor — nothing more!
(from the Tiger Book)

These photos show the fighting compartment of a Tiger. Above: The driver, the radioman and the loader; at right, the commander. All were linked by an intercom system.

Motto: Zur Leistung wird erst dann die Kraft, wenn sie zum rechten Ort geschafft:

C. Triebwerk

Das Wechselgetriebe ist ein hochgezüchtetes edles Reitpferd. Ein leichter Druck und es wechselt den Gang mit sicherer und schneller Selbstverständlichkeit. Du mußt es kunstgerecht pflegen und die Gestänge sauber einstellen, sonst bockt es wie ein Vollblüter, dessen Kandare falsch eingestellt und dessen Kinnkette schlecht verpaßt ist.

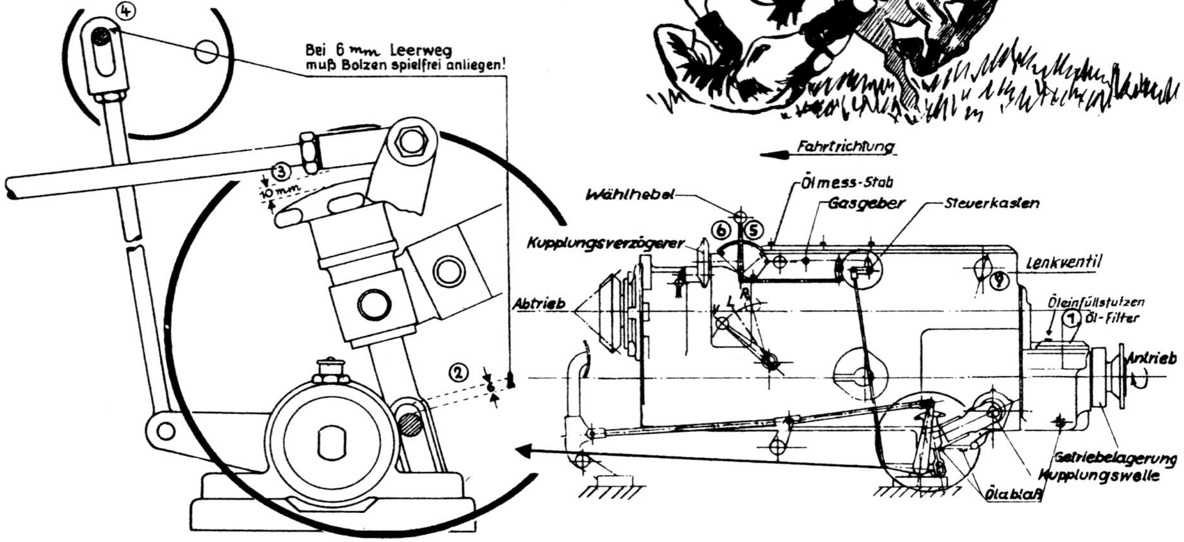

Above: A Tiger I at the invasion front in 1944 with three-color camouflage (sand-tan background with brown and green spots over it). In front is a VW Schwimmwagen.

Right: "A Tiger near Vitebsk on the big roadway" (Vitebsk-Moscow), also in 1944. It has the exhaust pipes of the later Tiger versions.

Upper right and next page: Two pages of the Tiger Book (D 656/27) as examples of its composition.

Motto: Selbst Meister messen. Denn Verlaß ist niemals auf das Augenmaß.

Das Messen

Wenn der Maler eine Strecke genau messen will, vergleicht er die Größe des Bleistiftes mit dem Modell.

Vergleiche Du die Größe des Stachels mit dem Ziel! Denn wenn Du weißt, wie groß Dein Ziel ist, kannst Du mit dem Strich ausrechnen, wie weit es entfernt ist.

Paß auf Die Russenpanzer sind alle 3 m breit. Nehmen wir an, er steht gerade so weit, daß er über 1¹/₂ Stachelzwischenräume reicht, dann sagst Du: „Aha!"

1¹/₂ Zwischenräume zu je 4 Strich = 6 Strich
6 Strich = 3 m
1 Strich = 3 : 6 = 0,5 m
0,5 m × 1000 = 500 m

Steht er über Eck, dann kannst Du mit Länge und Breite nicht rechnen, dann nimmst Du die Höhe. Der M 3 ist 3 m hoch. Nehmen wir an, in der Optik sieht es aus, wie auf der Zeichnung, dann rechnest Du:

3 Nebenstachelhöhen zu 2 Strich = 6 Strich
6 Strich = 3 m usw.

Im Fernrohr sieht die Stricheinteilung so aus:

Aufgabe: Rechne aus, wie weit dieser Lkw entfernt ist!

Hier ein paar Maße

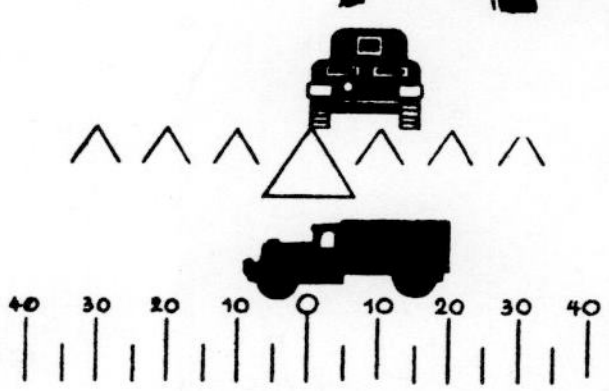

Moral: Schatz, statt wie weit's zum Ziele ist wieviel 's in Strich und Metern mißt. Die Meter teilst Du durch die Stricher, mal 1000 noch, dann mißt Du sicher.

Achtung! Die richtige Entfernung ist nicht das richtige Visier!

Above: Stopping to eat — the kitchen wagon has just come by and delivered the midday meal. Left: Two different eras meet.

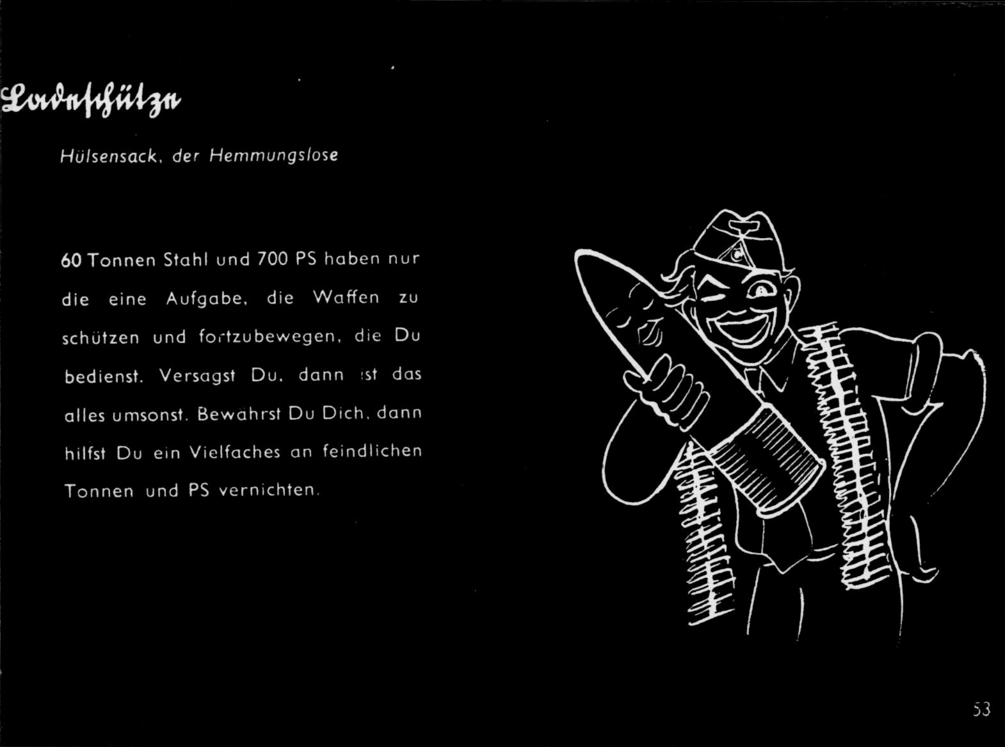

Ladeschütze

Hülsensack, der Hemmungslose

60 Tonnen Stahl und 700 PS haben nur die eine Aufgabe, die Waffen zu schützen und fortzubewegen, die Du bedienst. Versagst Du, dann ist das alles umsonst. Bewahrst Du Dich, dann hilfst Du ein Vielfaches an feindlichen Tonnen und PS vernichten.

53

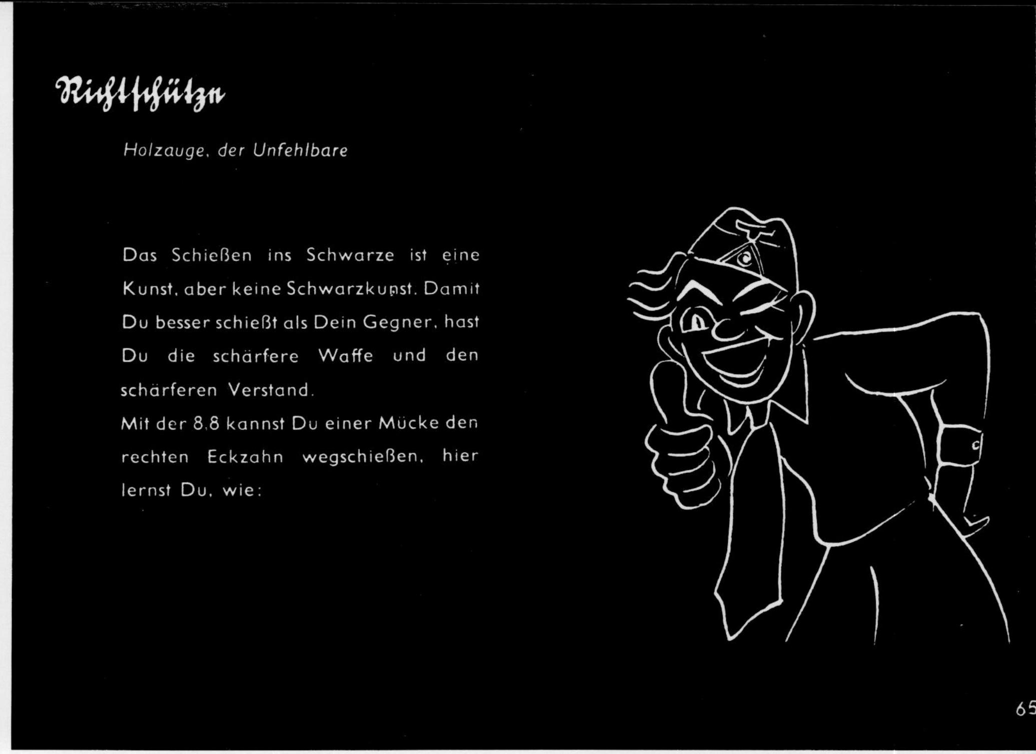

Richtschütze

Holzauge, der Unfehlbare

Das Schießen ins Schwarze ist eine Kunst, aber keine Schwarzkunst. Damit Du besser schießt als Dein Gegner, hast Du die schärfere Waffe und den schärferen Verstand.
Mit der 8.8 kannst Du einer Mücke den rechten Eckzahn wegschießen, hier lernst Du, wie:

65

Loader
Beanbag the Limitless
60 tons of steel and 700 horsepower have just one task: to protect and move the weapons that you operate. If you fail, then everything is in vain. If you prove yourself, then you help destroy a lot of enemy tons and horsepower.

Gunner
Wooden-eye the Infallible
Hitting the bull's-eye is an art, but not a black art. If you shoot better than your opponent, you have the sharper weapon and the sharper brain. With the 88 you can shoot away a flea's eye tooth. Here's where you learn how.

Above: Two more pictures from the Tiger Book. They show the title pages at the beginning of the descriptions of the loader's and gunner's work.

Technical service under Italy's olive trees.

The Repair Depot

Assembly cranes such as these can only be set up at the so-called repair depots in the back-line operations area far from the front. As can be seen (note the wheels), they were mobile cranes. Both pictures show the mounting of a turret. In the background is a Tiger with a good winter paint job.

Right page: Technical service and cleaning and mending time for this crew's Tiger and their equipment.

Left: A Tiger is being given a winter coat by primitive means (chalk and a root brush). Right: A Tiger above and a BMW motorcycle with sidecar, both with poor winter camouflage. It can be seen on the cycle that the former "paint" is almost all gone. On the other hand, the white sides of the field jackets (and hoods) are very effective — when they are new.

Here a Tiger has been given a good coat of winter paint — probably at a repair depot. The exhaust system and turret are not yet finished, though the former was generally not painted; it was not allowed on account of the heat. Note the Feifel ventilators on this Tiger, a sign that this Tiger was once intended for service in Africa.

Above and below: The end in the west (invasion front, 1944). Here a Tiger unit on the march was hit by carpet bombing in the narrow streets of a town in northern France. To what extent the tanks shown in these German photos could be repaired afterward is not known.

Right page: The end in the east.

Schiffer Military History

Schiffer Publishing Ltd.
4880 Lower Valley Road
Atglen, Pennsylvania 19310
Phone: (610) 593-1777 FAX: (610) 593-2002

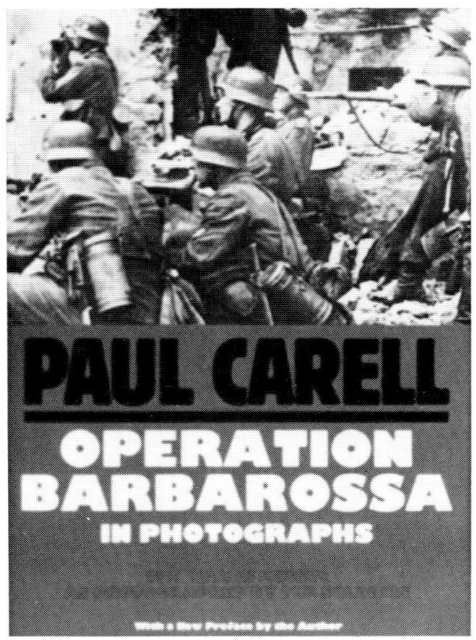